Art & Artist
Coffee Table Book
Mindful Creations
Edition 4

Anuragyam, New Delhi

Edition 4 : February 2025

Published by
Anuragyam, New Delhi
Website : www.anuragyam.com
Email : editor@anuragyam.com
Contact No. : +91-9999920037

Cover Design :
Er. Sachin Chaturvedi, Anuragyam

Printing & Marketing by: Notion Press
Distribution : Anuragyam, Notion Press

Why Do We Need Artists Coffee Table Book ??

In a world where the mundane often overshadows the extraordinary, where routine dulls our senses and where the beauty of everyday moments risks being overlooked, the Artists Coffee Table Book stands as a radiant beacon of inspiration. It serves as a heartfelt reminder of art's profound significance in our lives.

Imagine a universe where every stroke of a brush, every chord struck on a guitar and every word penned on a page tells the story of boundless human creativity. This book transcends being a mere collection of pretty pictures or abstract musings—it is a celebration of the human spirit, a vibrant chronicle of our shared journey through the intricate labyrinth of existence.

Within its pages, you'll encounter raw emotions laid bare on canvas, intricate dances of light and shadow immortalized through a photographer's lens and symphonies of color and form born from the minds of visionaries. Every turn of the page opens a doorway to a new world, inviting you to step outside your comfort zone and embrace the unfamiliar with awe.

But why, you might wonder, do we need such a book? Because in the chaos and clamor of modern life, we often lose touch with the sublime. We forget to pause, to breathe, to marvel at the wonders around us. The Artists Coffee Table Book serves as a gentle nudge—a call to arms for the soul—to recognize that beauty exists everywhere, often hidden in plain sight, waiting patiently for us to notice.

Art is not a luxury reserved for the elite; it is a vital language of the human experience. It transcends time, culture and circumstance. It is a mirror reflecting our deepest fears and desires, a bridge connecting us to one another and a compass guiding us toward meaning and purpose.

This book is more than a collection; it is a sanctuary for the weary soul. A refuge from the noise of the world, it allows us to lose ourselves in the enchanting realms born of imagination. It offers solace, inspiration and hope—a reminder that even in the darkest of times, beauty endures, unyielding.

So why do we need Artists Coffee Table Books? Because they remind us of who we are, where we've been and where we're destined to go. They awaken dormant senses, ignite our passions and rekindle the spark of creativity within us. These books are not just objects; they are portals to infinite possibilities, guiding us on transformative journeys of self-discovery and enlightenment.

PREFACE

Art is not merely a medium of expression but also the cradle of culture. Every individual or collective devoted to its elevation deserves profound admiration. Art has always been an echo of human consciousness, a tangible expression of intangible emotions. With each stroke of a brush, a fragment of the artist's soul is embedded onto the canvas, giving birth to a world that transcends boundaries. "Mindful Creations," in its fourth edition, stands as a reflection to this unyielding spirit of artistic expression, presenting a curated selection of fifty exquisite artworks by twenty-five remarkable artists. Published under the aegis of Anuragyam, New Delhi, this collection serves as an artistic odyssey, celebrating the rich and diverse spectrum of creativity that embodies our contemporary visual culture.

The artworks featured in this edition traverse multiple artistic realms, from the evocative figuration of Dr. Renuka Iyer, Inderjeet Kaur, KHR Priyanka Kumara, Bhavika Agrawal, Rajiv Kapoor, Anu Saxena, Avigyan Bhattacharya, Dr. Kukil Sharma and Krishan Kumar, to the lyrical semi-figuration brought to life by Mini Subhod, Nandita Singh, Simmi Kapoor, Priti Srivastava and Jyoti Prasad. Each artist, in their unique visual language, bridges the gap between realism and abstraction, intertwining narratives that speak to both the personal and the universal.

The fluidity and ethereal beauty of watercolor, mastered by Dr. Yatindra Mahobe, invite the viewer into a world where light and color breathe together in harmony. In contrast, the precision and intensity of graphite, as exemplified by Anju Daga and Vanshika, showcase a monochromatic depth that highlights intricate details and masterful shading. Ram Awasthi's historical artwork provides a profound exploration of our collective past, capturing moments steeped in time and tradition.

Modern art, with its audacious spirit and groundbreaking perspectives, finds a stronghold in the works of Subrata Chatterjee, Ram Krishna Agrawal, Vibhav Kshitiz and Mandira Ganguly. Their compositions challenge convention, inviting viewers to experience art beyond the constraints of form and representation. Meanwhile, Rakesh Verma's abstract expressions push the boundaries of perception, evoking emotions that transcend language and form, resonating with the core of human experience.

In "Mindful Creations," each page turns into a conversation—between artist and observer, between past and present, between the tangible and the imagined. The careful juxtaposition of styles, techniques and philosophies in this volume is not merely an exhibition but a meditation on the infinite possibilities of artistic interpretation. As an art writer and reviewer, I have had the privilege of witnessing how these brilliant minds channel their vision into compositions that not only captivate the eye but also stir the soul.

This fourth edition is a milestone, reinforcing Anuragyam's commitment to fostering artistic excellence. As you immerse yourself in the pages of this book, may you find inspiration, contemplation and a renewed appreciation for the limitless horizons of art. Let "Mindful Creations" be a sanctuary where imagination meets mindfulness and where every artwork serves as a window into a world of profound beauty and creative fervor.

I trust that this carefully assembled collection of visuals will captivate and inspire both connoisseurs and readers alike. My heartfelt felicitations to all the artists and collaborators whose creativity graces these pages.

Ram Prawesh Paul
International Artist & Educator
Art Writer & Reviewer
Author of Art Book : Samakaleen Kala
(Published by Lalit Kala Akademi, New Delhi)

5th Feb 2024

Message

Art is not just an expression—it is a heartbeat, a rhythm that connects souls across time and space. The Art & Artist Coffee Table Book is more than a collection of pages; it is a living, breathingreflection to the boundless world of creativity, where every brushstroke whispers a story and every sculpture holds the weight of a thousand emotions. It is not merely a book— it is an odyssey, an immersive journey into the depths of artistic brilliance, human resilience and the unyielding spirit of imagination. In this moment of reflection and gratitude, my heart swells with appreciation for Mrs. Mamta Rajak, whose unwavering belief in this vision has been the foundation of its success. Her support has not just lifted this endeavor; it has infused it with the strength and purpose that every great creation requires. Without her, this symphony of creativity, passion and inspiration could not have reached the heights it now embraces. I would also like to thank Mrs. Anju Daga for her support to us. Excellence is not granted; it is forged. It is shaped by hands that refuse to surrender, by minds that dare to dream and by souls that seek to redefine the boundaries of creative expression. This belief is at the core of everything we do at Anuragyam—we are not just publishers; we are storytellers, dream-weavers and custodians of artistic legacies. With each book we craft, we pledge to honor the trust placed in us. May this book ignite your imagination, stir your soul and remind you that art is not just something we create; it is something we become. With deepest gratitude and unwavering commitment.

Er. Sachin Chaturvedi
Founder, Anuragyam

28th Jan 2025

Message

As I turn the pages of Mindful Creations: Artistic Book, I find myself transported back to a time when my hands were steady with purpose and my heart beat in rhythm with every stroke of the brush. The scent of paint, the rough texture of canvas beneath my fingertips, the quiet hum of a world lost in creation—those moments live on in my soul, even as my hands now rest, content in their journey. Today, I celebrate you, the visionary behind this extraordinary book and the arrival of its third edition. Your dedication to the boundless world of art is nothing short of remarkable. Through these pages, you have not merely documented creativity—you have breathed life into it. You have given voice to those who see the world differently, who feel colors more deeply, who find poetry in the silent dance of light and shadow. As I read, I see not just techniques and insights but the raw pulse of passion, the echoes of every artist who has ever dared to dream. Your work is more than guidance—it is a lantern in the hands of those who wander the labyrinth of creation, seeking their own artistic truth. It reassures them, inspires them and reminds them that art is not about perfection—it is about heart, about courage, about the stories only they can tell. With this third edition, you extend your legacy further, casting ripples into the future. The brush may leave the hand, the chisel may rest, but the spirit of creation endures, passed from one soul to another, like an unbroken thread of light. So, from an artist whose hands may have stilled but whose heart still beats in color—I thank you. Congratulations on this magnificent achievement. May your book continue to awaken dreams, nurture visions and keep the fire of creativity burning for generations to come.

Dr. Dhruva Tiwari
Advisor, Anuragyam

31st Jan 2025

Message

Within the heart of this mesmerizing book, Anuragyam extends an invitation to step into a world where art breathes, dreams unfold and emotions find their truest expression. This journey is not just about colors on a canvas or strokes of genius—it is about souls who dared to create, voices that refused to be silenced and visions that reshaped the world of art. From the hands of masterful legends to the spirits of rising stars, these 25 extraordinary artists have woven magic through their craft. Each creation holds whispers of inspiration, each stroke areflection to resilience and each masterpiece a gateway into the artist's deepest emotions. Their works challenge the ordinary, urging us to see the unseen, feel the unspoken and embrace the unconventional. With every turn of the page, immerse yourself in a symphony of colors, emotions and thought-provoking narratives that linger long after the last image fades from sight. Experience the raw energy of abstract expressionists, where intuition takes the lead and emotions explode into breathtaking compositions. Wander through landscapes where nature speaks through the artist's hands. Serene meadows, storm-kissed oceans, golden sunsets—all captured with a reverence that transforms the ordinary into the extraordinary. In these breathtaking depictions, art and nature become one, whispering of the timeless beauty that surrounds us. As this journey through Mindful Creations comes to a close, may these stories and masterpieces ignite something within you—a spark of inspiration, a surge of creativity, a longing to express your own soul through art. For in the world of creation, there are no limits, no rules—only the boundless freedom of imagination. May these artists leave an everlasting imprint on your heart, guiding you toward your own artistic destiny.

Taruna Mathur

Dr. Taruna Mathur
Principal Investigator
Anuragyam

ARTISTS

Preface   Mr. Ram Prawesh Paul, International Artist & Educator
Founder   Er. Sachin Chaturvedi, Founder, Anuragyam , New Delhi,
Advisor   Dr. Dhruva Tiwari, International Artist, Raaipur Chhattisgarh
Message   Dr. Taruna Mathur, International Artist & PI at Anuragyam, Vadodara, Gujarat

AVIGYAN BHATTACHARYA
Thane, Maharashtra

Avigyan Bhattacharya is a renowned visual artist, tech YouTuber and academically accomplished scholar whose ambition and achievements set him apart especially for his age. Currently pursuing an MSc in International Business at the University of Birmingham Dubai he has consistently demonstrated excellence in academics ranking among the top performers in his CBSE Class 10 and 12 board examinations. His artistic journey began at the age of 13 with a solo art exhibition in Muscat which earned immense appreciation from visitors and media marking the start of a stellar career.

Over the years he has participated in numerous exhibitions and competitions across Muscat Dubai Mumbai Delhi and Pune earning significant recognition and awards often outshining seasoned professionals in the art fraternity.

Avigyan's accolades include prestigious awards like the Oman-in-Their-Eyes Award (2015) Ratan-e-Hind Awards (2018 and 2019) Swami

DEFIANCE
Medium: Oil on Canvas : Size:26.7 x 44.9 Inch

EUPHORIA
Medium: Oil on Canvas : Size: 30.7 x 40.5 Inch

Vivekananda Excellence Award (2019) Youth of India Award (2019) International Kalaratnam Award (2020) and First Prize in the Overall Portrait Category by Absolute Arts (2021) among many others.

His exceptional talent has also been acknowledged by prominent international agencies such as World Genius Records The British World Records and the India Book of Records for setting records in the number of art exhibitions and awards achieved as a teenager.

Additionally he has been featured in notable platforms including the Top 100 Contemporary Artists book in Dubai the Startale Book of emerging contemporary artists and The Paintbrush Community website.

Avigyan's journey reflects his passion dedication and extraordinary talent as he continues to excel as an artist YouTuber and scholar inspiring young talents across the globe.

ANU SAXENA
Singapore

The Artist Who Breathes Life into Canvas & Where Engineering Precision Meets Artistic Whimsy. Step into the mesmerizing world of Anu Saxena, a visionary artist renowned for her unparalleled talent in hyper-realistic human portraits. With the stroke of a brush and the precision of a pencil, Anu captures the essence of her subjects, bringing them to life on canvas in exquisite detail. Her mastery extends to the rich depth of oil paintings and the delicate finesse of pencil sketching, showcasing a diverse range of skills that elevate her artistry to new heights.

The artist weaves a vibrant tapestry that harmonizes the disciplined world of engineering with the boundless realm of artistic expression. Within the confines of her studio, she engineer, a delightful convergence of the cerebral and the

UNTITLED SERIES
Medium: Oil & Acrylic Colour : Size: 16.5 x 23.4 Inch

STILL LIFE RENDERING
Medium: Oil & Acrylic Colour : Size: 16.5 x 23.4 Inch

creative, infusing each piece with a touch of humor and a dash of whimsy. Not content with simply creating art for herself, Anu Saxena generously opens her talents to the world, offering commission paintings that speak directly to the hearts of her clients. Whether immortalizing cherished memories or capturing the essence of loved ones, Anu's commissioned pieces stand asreflections to her ability to infuse each work with boundless emotion and beauty.

Beyond her own creations, Anu Saxena dedicates herself to nurturing the artistic spirit in others. With a passion for teaching, she imparts her knowledge and expertise to aspiring artists of all ages, guiding them on a transformative journey of creative exploration and skill development. From young minds to seasoned adults, Anu's guidance empowers each individual to unlock their potential and express themselves through the captivating language of art. In the world of Anu Saxena, every stroke and shading is a reflection to her unwavering dedication to artistry and a celebration of the boundless possibilities of human expression.

VANSHIKA
Hansi, Haryana

Vanshika, a self-taught artist from India, has carved a distinctive niche in the art world through her unwavering passion for creativity and self-expression. With a mastery of sketching and painting, her art resonates with depth, emotion and an extraordinary vision that continues to captivate audiences.

Her artistic journey is a reflection to relentless dedication and an insatiable curiosity for exploring the vast landscapes of visual art. From traditional forms to contemporary aesthetics, Vanshika's creations transcend boundaries, offering viewers a profound and personal dialogue through her brushstrokes and sketches. Vanshika's talent has graced prestigious platforms, both national and international. She showcased her artistic brilliance at the Ayodhyaa Kala Sanskriti Mahakumbh, a celebration of India's rich artistic heritage and the

OLD WOMAN
Medium: Pencile Sketch : Size: 11.7 x 16.5 Inch

RAM & PM MODI
Medium: Pencile Sketch : Size: 11.7 x 16.5 Inch

Aagman National Art Workshop, where she collaborated with other visionary artists, further expanding her creative horizons. The year 2023 marked a milestone in Vanshika's career, as she clinched the first prize in Rangakash, an international sketching competition that celebrated her exceptional talent. Additionally, her third-place victory in the 5th Child International Art Competition underscored her ability to connect with audiences across diverse age groups. Her work, featured in the prestigious Kalayatra magazine, further solidified her standing in the art community. Vanshika's contributions to Viksit Bharat, an event organized by the National Gallery of Modern Art and the Government of India, highlight her commitment to enriching India's cultural narrative. Through themes that explore identity, nature and society, she crafts visual stories that challenge perceptions and ignite introspection. As Vanshika continues to evolve, her vision is clear: to inspire and transform through art. With every stroke and shade, she reminds the world of art's unparalleled power to heal, connect and elevate. Undoubtedly, Vanshika is a rising luminary in the art world, poised to leave an indelible mark on the canvas of history.

VIBHAV KSHITIZ
New Delhi

Vibhav is a multifaceted creative force—a painter, author and poet whose work resonates with a unique fusion of cubism, expressionism and impressionism. His art, deeply personal and evocative, draws from profound life experiences, including near-death encounters that have profoundly shaped his outlook on existence. What distinguishes Vibhav's artistry is his narrative-driven approach. He believes every painting carries a story waiting to be told and ensures his audience never struggles to interpret his vision. As he aptly puts it, "What is the worth of an idea if not interpreted in a way that preserves the original intention?" Beyond crafting visual masterpieces, Vibhav extends his creativity to guiding collectors on how to incorporate his art into their lives. Whether considering aesthetics, psychology, philosophy, or even Vastu principles, he ensures that each artwork enhances its surroundings on multiple levels. His creations transcend mere visual appeal; they are reflections of his inner journey and thoughts. From the vast cosmos to the fragile beauty of a flower, his

A SEPARATION : Medium : Acrylic : Size : 30 x 30 Inch

AN ATTACHMENT : Medium : Acrylic : Size : 30 x 30 Inch

art invites viewers to delve deeper into the nuances of life. Through his platform, artwordvibhav.com, Vibhav shares his paintings, poetry and books with a global audience, blending his artistic vision with his literary talent. Vibhav's academic background—a Bachelor's degree in Business Finance from Jamia Millia Islamia and a Postgraduate Diploma in Marketing Management from the All India Management Association—equips him with the skills to balance his creative pursuits with business acumen. Looking to the future, Vibhav envisions collaborations with architects, designers, galleries and curators across India and beyond, striving to make his art more accessible to audiences worldwide. Outside of his professional sphere, Vibhav enjoys exploring the world through cinema and travel and remains committed to philanthropic causes. He currently resides in Delhi with his family, continuing to inspire and captivate through his artistic journey.

BHAVIKA AGRAWAL
Noida, Uttar Pradesh

Bhavika is a passionate artist whose creative spirit finds its expression through the delicate strokes of color pencils. For Bhavika, art is more than a hobby—it is a sacred journey, a cornerstone of her life that allows her to convey profound emotions, devotion and the beauty of the divine.

At the heart of Bhavika's artistry lies an unwavering devotion to Lord Radhakrishnan. Each portrait is a heartfelt homage to the timeless grace, teaching and serenity of Lord Krishna. Through vibrant hues and intricate details. She captures the divine beauty and spiritual essence that inspire a sense of peace, joy and reflection in the hearts of viewers.

Her art work extends beyond Krishna's portraits to celebrate the sacred symbolism of Kamdhenu the divine cow revered in Hindu mythology as a symbol of abundance, prosperity and divine grace. Bhavika's art explores the

KAMDHENU GOW MATA
Medium : Colour Pencils : Size : A4 Sheet - 8.3 X 11.7 Inch

PEACE OF MIND
Medium : Colour Pencils : Size : A3 Sheet - 11.7 X 16.5 Inch

harmonious connection between Kamdhenu and Radhakrishnan, weaving a rich narrative of spiritual abundance and divine unity. Every creation is a labor of love and meticulous craftsmanship. With careful blending and shading, she brings life to intricate details that transform their art into a medium of spiritual storytelling. Her compositions radiate a soulful energy, inviting viewers to pause, reflect and connect with the divine. Through their art. She believes in the transformative power of creativity to inspire, uplift and forge meaningful spiritual connections. Each piece is not just a reflection of their devotion but also an invitation to others to experience the beauty and serenity of divine expression. With every stroke, Bhavika shares a piece of her soul, creating art that soothes, fulfills and transcends the ordinary.

DR. YATINDRA MAHOBE
Narsinghpur, Madhya Pradesh

Welcome to the vibrant world of artistic expression of Dr. Yatindra Mahode where every stroke tells a story and every hue speaks volumes. It is with great pleasure that Anuragyam introduces you to the extraordinary journey of an artist whose passion for creativity knows no bounds.

From the tender years of childhood, art has been a constant companion for our featured artist. His earliest memories are painted with sketches of heroes, heroines, and tales woven from the pages of cherished books.

Hailing from the serene landscapes of Malanjkhand, District Balaghat, Madhya Pradesh, his artistic odyssey took root and blossomed into a remarkable career.

His unwavering dedication to fine arts led him to pursue a Bachelor's

GRAND MAA WITH ME
Medium : Watercolour on Paper : Size : 15 x 20 Inch

OLD MAN
Medium : Watercolour on Paper : Size : 12 x 16 Inch

and Master's degree from the esteemed Indira Kala Sangeet Vishwavidyalaya, Khairagarh, Chhattisgarh.

His journey of learning and exploration culminated in a Ph.D. from Rani Durgavati University, Jabalpur, in 2013 — an affirmation of his commitment to artistic excellence.

Since 2004, as an Assistant Professor of Painting at Government Women's College, Narsinghpur, Madhya Pradesh, he has not only nurtured aspiring artists but has also evolved as a creator, earning numerous accolades and exhibiting his work on international platforms.

His art stands as a testament to talent, perseverance and an unyielding love for creative expression.

n recent years, his artistic soul has found solace in the fluidity of watercolors and the textured depth of collages.

Capturing the essence of rural life with transparency and finesse, they masterfully embrace the challenges of these intricate mediums, infusing each piece with emotion and purpose.

DR. (HON.) RENUKA IYER
Babusapalya, Bangalore

Born in Chennai and now based in Bangalore, my journey as an artist has been shaped by a unique upbringing across India, thanks to my father's service in the Air Force.

This constant exposure to diverse landscapes and cultures enriched my artistic soul, fueling my passion for creativity. Drawing and painting are gifts I embraced early, beginning at the age of 5 and refining my craft to mastery by 18.

I am skilled in a variety of mediums, including watercolors, poster colors, color pencils, graphite, oil paints, acrylics and inks. Each medium allows me to explore and express different facets of my creativity.

My fascination with art extends to exploring Traditional, Folk, Tribal, Contemporary, Fusion, Abstract and Mandala forms—each inspired

COSMIC SHIVA - AMRITH & VISH
Medium: Acrylic Paints : Size: 24 x 30

SHRINATHJI FULL MOON DARSHAN
Medium: Acrylic Paints : Size: 20 x 24 Inch

by the cultural diversity I've encountered throughout my life. Nature plays a profound role in my artistic inspiration, offering endless beauty and lessons that I strive to capture in my work.

With a Bachelor's in Fine Arts from Shantanu Chitra Vidyalaya, I have had the privilege of training under some of the finest masters. I learned the intricate Mysore Traditional Painting from Subramanyam Raju of Karnataka Chitrakala Parishath and Ganjifa Miniature Painting from National Award winner Raghupathy Bhatt.

Over the years, I've showcased my work in numerous exhibitions, both online and offline, earning recognition and accolades as an eminent artist. Today, I specialize in Traditional, Folk and Tribal art forms, with a focus on their historical and cultural significance.

My mission is clear—to bring India's rich artistic heritage to the global stage. Through my art, I aim to connect people with the stories, traditions and beauty of our culture, spreading its essence across the world with authenticity and passion.

ANJU DAGA
Bhadohi, Uttar Pradesh

Anju Daga stands as a luminary in the realm of artistry, her graphite pencile strokes weaving narratives that captivate the soul. Hailing from the quaint town of Bhadohi in Uttar Pradesh, India, Anju's journey as an artist spans over two decades, marked by innovation, skill and an unwavering passion for her craft. Specializing in portraits and diverse painting forms on paper & canvas, she has earned international acclaim for her exceptional talent. Through-out her illustrious career, Anju has graced numerous offline and online art exhibitions with her exquisite creations, each piece areflection to her boundless creativity. Her works have not only adorned galleries but have also graced the pages of prestigious magazines, resonating with audiences worldwide. Anju's artistic prowess extends beyond mere exhibition participation, as evidenced by the array of accolades adorning her illustrious career.

CHOTI SI AASHA
Medium : Graphite : Size : 16 x 23 Inch

HOURSE POWER
Medium : Graphite : Size : 48 x 30 Inch

From the coveted Vande Mataram Award 2024 by Anuragyam, New Delhi, to the Influencer Woman Award, bestowed upon her twice, her mantle shines with recognition. With over 35 medals garnered from various online art competitions and the esteemed honor of being named one of the Top 25 Best Artists of India by the Indian Art Factory, Anju's accolades speak volumes of her unparalleled talent. Yet, perhaps most esteemed among her accomplishments are the Rabindra Nath Tagore Kala Samman Award and the IAF Annual Award 2024, where she was bestowed with the title of Kala Bhushan. These prestigious honors serve as areflection to Anju's indelible mark on the art world, solidifying her status as a true luminary. Beyond her artistic endeavors, Anju Daga balances her passion with the role of a homemaker, epitomizing the essence of a modern-day Renaissance woman. Her journey stands as an inspiration, showcasing the transformative power of art and the boundless potential within the human spirit. Anju Daga, with her unparalleled talent and unwavering dedication, continues to enrich the world with the beauty of her creations, leaving an indelible imprint on the paper & canvas of artistic expression.

RAM AWASTHI
Mumbai, Maharashtra

From Corporate corridors to the vibrant world of art, Ram Awasthi embodies the resilience and creative spirit that often lies dormant, waiting for the opportune moment to flourish.

His trajectory, marked by a childhood pas-sion for art, was momentarily obscured by the pursuit of commerce during his college years.

Yet, adversity often serves as a catalyst for transformation and it was amidst the solitude of the 2020 Covid lockdown that the dormant artist within him stirred to life. Ram Awasthi draws inspiration from ancient heritage structure , his canvas becomes a reflection of the city's dynamic architectural landscape.

However, his artistic palette extends beyond mere structures; it embraces the kaleidoscope of customs and traditions that define the cultural tapestry of India. With each stroke of the brush, he brings to life the vibrant hues of Indian culture , weaving tales of its rich heritage into his artwork.

AAFSANA
Medium : Acrylic on Canvas : Size : 24 X 36 Inch

IBAADAT
Medium : Acrylic on Canvas : Size : 30 X 36 Inch

Nurturing his passion, Ram Awasthi has ventured into a myriad of mediums, exploring the expressive possibilities of oil, acrylics and beyond. His studio, aptly named "Art Connects Studio," situated in the heart of Vile Parle East, Mumbai, serves as a sanctuary where creativity knows no bounds. The recognition garnered by Ram Awasthi is areflection to his artistic prowess, with a diverse clientele ranging from art enthusiasts to corporate establishments.

His work graces both private collections and public spaces, bridging the gap between artistic expression and societal engagement. In Ram Awasthi, we witness not just an artist, but a storyteller whose canvases resonate with the vibrancy of life itself. With each creation, he invites us to journey alongside him, to explore the intersection of art and identity in a world brimming with color and possibility.

His Exhibitions Contemporary Art Show at Jehangir Art Gallery, Nepal Art Council - Kathmandu 2023, World Art Dubai , Lalit Kala Academy Lucknow and Delhi, Bombay Art Society 2024, World Art Dubai, New York Art Expo 2025

SUBRATA CHATTERJEE
Kolkata, West Bengal

Born in Kolkata, 1978, Subrata, brought up in the suburbs, Barasat Town near Kolkata, always tries to quench his thirst from his circumference, trying to catch the baroque beauty of nature with its inner charm and spontaneous melody.

The deep calm flow of death is taking an eternal journey. The dense 'tamisra' that came between adolescence and youth suddenly took a turn into the realm of line and colours. It is an obscure but core luminary strata. In the world of occult enchanting, human psyche reacts differently. Subrata's journey into the world of art and aesthetics started with this understanding. 'Art opens the window of spirit to get the nectar of life' and it came to his life at the very dawn of his childhood as a gift from Mita and Prankrishna. Later it was shaped at his Art College's days. Colour and chiaroscuro, space and sangfroid,

SURRENDER
Medium : Ink Jottings with Acrylic Wash on Paper : Size : 10 x 13 Inch

PIOUS : Medium : Heavy Body Acrylic on Ground Paper : Size : 11.5 X 12 Inch

perception and perseverance give him a call to be deeply engrossed in. Stories of his fading down memory lane and the grey melancholy of his mother's final journey re-appear with mysterious hues and shades. Enigmatic and grey palette ensnares him to be a part of this play and makes him discover an uncanny world, where his silent journey wants to meet. Middle tones play a magic in his imaginations with different shades of brown, ochres, black and blues.

Integrity of artistic spirit and an occult celebration of colours is soul of his paintings. It helps to elevate the mind unto a mystic plane. The transformation of exterior to inner is the core of his works. Earning numerous recognitions, merits and awards, he carries his own quiet, luminary and meditative world within, transcripts lines and hues. Now, he is a full time painter _ experimenting with methods in his en-plein air and subjective paintings.

RAM KRISHNA
AGRAWAL
Noida, Uttar Pradesh

Ram Krishna Agrawal, a science graduate by education, has carved an extraordinary path in the world of fashion and art. His journey began in the fashion industry, where he steadily rose from a designer to an industry expert. Yet, beyond his professional pursuits, Agrawal found his true calling in the realm of art and painting—a passion that has shaped his life and creative vision. A self-taught artist, Agrawal's artistic exploration began with abstract forms, drawing inspiration from the revolutionary works of Picasso. Over time, his style evolved, blending India's traditional folk and tribal art forms—such as Madhubani and Gond—with his unique contemporary touch. By infusing these age-old traditions with his distinct vision, he breathes vibrant new life into India's artistic heritage. Using a versatile range of mediums, including watercolors, acrylics and pens, Agrawal's works seamlessly bridge the gap between the contemporary and the traditional. His art not only celebrates India's cultural richness but also redefines it for modern audiences. Agrawal's mission

FOREST : Medium : Water Colour & Pen : Size : 11 x 8.5 Inch

TRAVELLERS : Medium : Water Colour & Pens: Size : 11 x 8.5 Inch

is profound: to showcase the beauty and depth of India's heritage to the world, innovatively combining time-honored techniques with modern interpretations. Agrawal's creations have garnered widespread recognition, earning him acclaim and accolades on numerous platforms. Yet, for him, painting transcends accolades; it is his sanctuary and therapy. Art, to Agrawal, is a universal language that fosters harmony, healing and understanding across societal divides. Deeply inspired by his mother, an unrecognized artist whose creativity adorned their home, Agrawal's work is a tribute to her legacy. Through his art, he seeks not just to gain recognition but to spread peace, love and the enduring beauty of India's cultural tapestry. For Ram Krishna Agrawal, art is not merely a profession—it is a heartfelt mission to inspire and connect humanity. Honored as an India Book of Records holder in 2024 for his artistic achievements.

INDERJEET KAUR
Mohali, Punjab

Painting is more than a passion for me; it is the essence of my being. My love for oil colors has sparked a dream to become a skilled portrait artist, while my work in landscapes allows me to explore new techniques and push creative boundaries. For me, art is a lifeline, a healing force that keeps me grounded through life's struggles. While I am an interior designer by profession and a fashion designer by choice, I am an artist at heart. Creativity unites all these fields, making art my sanctuary and a constant source of inspiration. Engaging in creative work has been my refuge, turning challenging times into moments of joy and self-discovery. Over the years, I've earned recognition and prestigious awards for my artistry. These include the Bronze Award in the 9th Future Star Artist 2nd National Online Art Exhibition by Manikarnika Art Gallery, the Diamond Achievement Award, the Outstanding Artist Award by

LAKE VEIW
Medium : Oil on Canvas : Size : 20 X 18 Inch

GANGUBAI : Medium : Oil on Canvas : Size : 10 X 10 Inch

Dream Paintbrush, the Bhartiya Kala Ratna Art Achiever Award and the Rabindranath Tagore Kala Samman Award by Ajanta Ellora International Art Gallery. Additionally, I've received the Top Oil Color Work Winner Award by Vibhu Art Zone and the Picasso Award by BM Art Gallery. I've also showcased my work in numerous group exhibitions across India, such as the Blockbuster Art Exhibition in Delhi, The Flamboyant Event at Jawahar Kala Kendra in Jaipur, Colorful Saga at Lokayata Art Gallery in South Delhi and Artistry Unleashed in Goa. My international exhibitions include the Haat of Art in Delhi, Parindo Ki Udaan in Punjab Kala Bhawan and the FAG International Art Exhibition in Shimla. My last few exhibitions were held in Chandigarh and Amritsar. A group art exhibition took place in October at the Government Art Gallery, Sector 10, Chandigarh. The second exhibition was held in November in Amritsar. Later in November, another group exhibition was organized at the Government Art Gallery, Sector 10. This month, I have an upcoming group show in December.

K.H.R PRIYANKARA KUMARA
Gampaha, Sri Lanka

From the vibrant landscapes of Kegalle, Sri Lanka, to the halls of artistic academia, my journey as an artist has been areflection to passion, dedication and relentless pursuit of creativity. Gifted with an innate talent for art from a young age, I began honing my skills during my schooling years at KG/ Kegalu Maha Vidyalaya, Kegalle. My path led me to the prestigious University of Visual and Performing Arts in Colombo, where I delved deeply into the realms of painting, sculpture, graphic art, printmaking and abstract art.

Chosen to specialize in European academic art, I spent six transformative years exploring its intricacies, culminating in earning a Special Bachelor of Fine Arts (SBFA) degree. My education instilled in me a profound appreciation for the timeless works of masters like

FATHER'S LOVE
Medium: Creyon (Pastal) on Paper(Realistic) : Size: 11.7 x 16.5 Inch

PATIENCE
Medium: Water Colour on Paper(Realistic) : Size: 11.7 x 16.5 Inch

Leonardo da Vinci and Raphael Sanzio, whose use of theoretical colors continues to inspire my artistic journey.

Balancing a dual identity as a professional artist and educator, I joined Rathnavali Balika Vidyalaya in Gampaha as an art teacher, a role I passionately fulfill to this day. Equipped with a Postgraduate Diploma in Education (PGDE), I've dedicated myself to nurturing young minds while continuing to evolve my own artistic pursuits.

My artistic focus lies in realistic academic paintings, enriched by experimentation with diverse mediums, particularly pastel. Inspired by the interplay of colors in classical masterpieces, I push the boundaries of pastel painting, exploring new techniques to breathe life into my creations.

Over the years, my art has found its voice through numerous exhibitions, where each piece reflects a blend of tradition, innovation and my love for vibrant, expressive color palettes. For me, art is not just a profession— it is a lifelong passion, a journey of exploration and a bridge between the past and the future of creativity.

MINI SUBOTH
Thane West, Maharashtra

She stands as a luminary in the world of contemporary painting, celebrated for her extraordinary talent and the emotional resonance her works evoke. With each stroke of her brush, she creates a vivid symphony of modern aesthetics and deep artistic expression, crafting a visual language that speaks to the soul.

From a young age, Mini's passion for art has been a guiding force, shaping her journey into a celebrated artist with a style uniquely her own. Her paintings, characterized by bold brushstrokes, vibrant hues and the masterful play of light and shadow, transport viewers into a world brimming with depth and emotion.

Her latest collection is a reflection to her artistic evolution, presenting a series of breathtaking works that narrate stories rooted in human emotions and experiences. Each painting is a window into Mini's perspective on life—an exploration of love, joy, sorrow and longing. Her ability to capture the raw essence of emotions through her dynamic brushwork and striking use

SANGAM DIP
Medium : Acrylic on Canvas : Size : 23.5 X 35 Inch

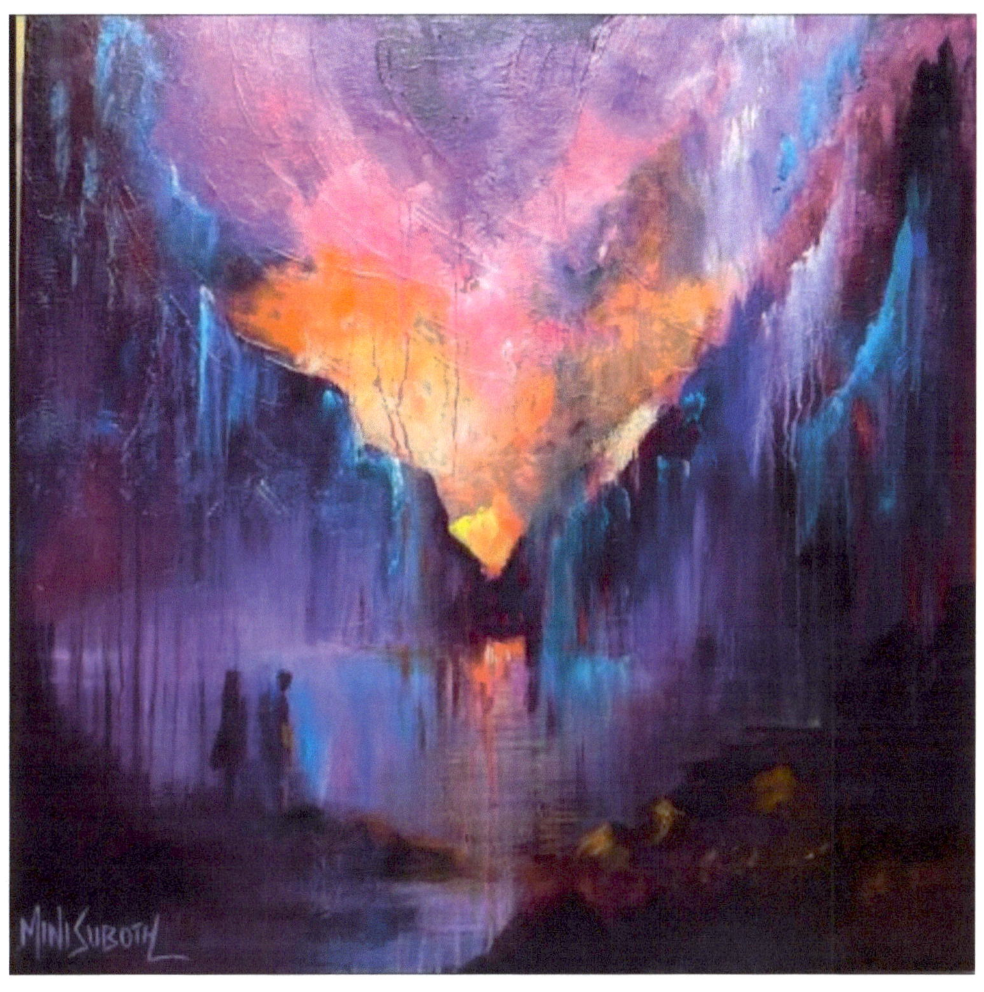

PUREST PORTAL
Medium : Acrylic on Canvas : Size : 35 X 35 Inch

of color leaves an indelible impact on all who encounter her art. Drawing inspiration from the beauty of nature, the richness of diverse cultures and the intricacies of human relationships, Mini's paintings serve as a mirror to her inner world. They are not merely visual creations but profound reflections of her thoughts and emotions, skillfully translated onto canvas. Her works have graced prestigious galleries and museums globally, earning critical acclaim and a devoted following among collectors and art enthusiasts. Featured in prominent publications, Mini Suboth has cemented her place as a trailblazer in contemporary art. Through her innovative approach and unwavering dedication, Mini continues to redefine the boundaries of artistic expression. Her paintings are more than masterpieces—they are profound journeys into the human experience, inspiring introspection and connecting hearts worldwide.

NANDITA SINGH
New Delhi

Hailing from the mesmerizing Blue City of Jodhpur, Rajasthan and now residing in New Delhi, Nandita is a professional artist whose passion for painting blossomed in childhood and flourished into a celebrated career.

Her artistic journey began at the age of 5, with her innate talent for painting and sketching paving the way for her creative future. Officially earning her Master's in Fine Arts in 2015, Nandita has been a force in the art world ever since.

What sets Nandita apart is her extraordinary versatility. From vivid sketches to intricate paintings, she effortlessly navigates various artistic mediums, breathing life into her creations.

Yet, her true muse lies in abstract art, where colors become her language—a powerful medium to express emotions, stories and ideas that transcend words.

For Nandita, art is more than a visual experience; it is a soulful connection.

AARYA
Medium : Acrylic on Canvas : Size : 24 X 36 Inch

SHIVSHAKTI YANTRA
Medium : Acrylic on Canvas : Size : 30 X 36 Inch

She believes every stroke of the brush and every splash of color carries an untold story, inviting viewers to embark on their own journeys of interpretation.

Her works have graced numerous prestigious exhibitions across North India, adorning the walls of renowned galleries and earning admiration from art connoisseurs and casual enthusiasts alike.

With a keen understanding of the evolving art world, Nandita actively participates in online exhibitions and competitions, showcasing her talent to a global audience and continually expanding her artistic reach.

Nandita's journey is one of dedication, passion and boundless creativity. Whether through physical exhibits or digital platforms, she continues to inspire and captivate with her mastery of colors and her ability to transform canvases into vibrant realms of imagination.

RAKESH VERMA
Bundi, Rajasthan

For over 20 years, this contemporary artist has been weaving magic on canvas, creating evocative works that transcend the ordinary.

His artistic journey began with figurative art, a realm he passionately explored for 18 years. During this phase, he brought to life a variety of themes through series such as Mother and Child, Various Forms of Women, Life of Ducks and even the dynamic energy of cricket as a subject. These creations brought him immense satisfaction, reflecting the depth of his artistic soul.

In 2022, a new chapter began as he embraced abstract art—a form that resonates deeply with his creative spirit. Immersed in the world of abstraction, he finds joy and fulfillment, living a truly blissful life of artistic exploration.

WAVES OF MIND
Medium: Acrylic Colour on Ivory Sheet : Size: 22 x 28 Inch

PATIENCE
Medium: Acrylic Colour on Ivory Sheet : Size: 22 x 28 Inch

With an impressive portfolio of over 60 group shows and four solo exhibitions, his works have garnered widespread recognition, earning him numerous awards and honors.

However, for this artist, the essence of art transcends accolades or commercial pursuits. Painting, for him, is not a commodity but a sacred act—a form of worship that brings profound happiness and spiritual connection.

Since 2013, he has been shaping the artistic minds of the next generation as an art teacher at Jawahar Navodaya Vidyalaya. Balancing his teaching career with his own practice, he remains dedicated to nurturing creativity in others while continuing to evolve as an artist.

Through his work, this artist exemplifies the power of passion and purpose, proving that art is not just a profession but a journey of self-discovery, joy and inspiration.

SIMMI KAPOOR
Noida, Uttar Pradesh

The colors of life are like a symphony, each hue contributing a unique note to the melody of our existence. Through the rich tapestry of tradition, we unravel threads connecting us to our roots—threads woven with stories of heritage, love and boundless creativity. For her, this connection is not just a practice but a meditation, a way to pour love into the world through the art of her hands, needles, threads and shimmering beads.

Every creation brings her immense joy, a reflection of her soul's dedication to preserving tradition and heritage. The appreciation she receives from those who find solace and connection in her art fuels her passion further, igniting the fire to keep exploring and creating.

She firmly believes that engaging with art is transformative, offering more than just an outlet for creativity. It cultivates mindfulness,

SOULMATE
Medium : Hand Embroidery : Size : 60 X 75 Inch

BEAUTY IN SIMPLICITY : Medium : Hand Embroidery : Size : 60 X 90 Inch

serving as a mirror that reflects our inner worlds and deepens our understanding of ourselves. Art becomes a bridge to self-awareness and inner peace, intertwining beauty and mental health in the most harmonious way.

As she often says, "Zindagi zinda dilli ka naam hai"—life is about living with passion and spirit. To her, passion is a compass, guiding her through the intricate journey of creativity. She believes age holds no barriers to dreaming and achieving. Every dream deserves a place in your life and every effort is a step toward that dream.

Her mantra is simple yet profound: Celebrate yourself, even when the world is silent. Be your harshest critic and your loudest cheerleader. After all, it's the blend of self-love and relentless determination that transforms life into a masterpiece. Let the symphony of your passion play on, vibrant and unrestrained!

PRITI SRIVASTAVA
Lucknow, Uttar Pradesh

Priti Srivastava, a luminary in Indian folk art, breathes life into tradition with her enchanting creations, often described as "folk tales on paper." Her mastery of art forms like Madhubani, Warli and Lippan allows her to blend heritage with modern aesthetics, crafting narratives that resonate across generations. Born in Balrampur, Uttar Pradesh, Priti's love for art was nurtured by her childhood immersed in folk festivals and craft fairs. However, it was a cultural festival in Agra that rekindled her passion, setting her on a transformative artistic journey in 2018.

Priti's paintings celebrate the everyday heroism of women, characterized by bold colors, intricate pen-work and evocative titles. Her works have graced prestigious exhibitions at venues like Lokayata Art Gallery, Lalit Kala Academy and

JALPARI (MADHUBANI PAINTING)
Medium: Using Handmade Paper & Acrylic Colors : Size: 14 x 16 Inch

PRATHA
Medium: Using Handmade Paper & Acrylic Colors : Size: 14 x 16 Inch

more. Recognized with accolades such as the Bharat Kala Gaurav Award, Amrita Shergill Kala Ratna Award and Asia Icon Award, her artistic brilliance is matched by her unwavering dedication, reflected in over 20 gold medals from national and international competitions. Through her art label, Pahee, Priti has not only turned her passion into a thriving career but has also inspired countless aspiring artists to persevere. A multifaceted talent, she is also a folk singer, composer and blogger

Her blog, Sanjhaa Bhor, celebrates folk music, while her compositions preserve India's rural melodies. Supported by her family, Priti beautifully balances her roles as a homemaker, artist and entrepreneur, ensuring India's folk traditions thrive in the modern world.

She contributed to a short film focused on raising election awareness, showcasing her versatility and creativity. Serving as a songwriter, music composer and actor, she played a pivotal role in bringing the project to life. Her lyrics and compositions added depth to the film's message, while her acting brought an engaging and relatable touch to the narrative.

RAJIV KAPOOR
Dehradun, Uttrakhand

After a fulfilling career with Oriental Insurance Company, Rajiv Kapoor embarked on a remarkable new journey—one that celebrates passion, self-discovery and the limitless possibilities of life's second innings. What began as a quiet retirement has transformed into a kaleidoscope of creativity, as Rajiv embraced the world of painting with open arms and an eager heart. For years, the artist within Rajiv lay dormant, quietly nudging him as he navigated the structured demands of a corporate life. Retirement became the perfect canvas to finally answer this call. Armed with a brush and an innate curiosity, he plunged into a realm of vibrant colors and bold strokes, weaving dreams onto blank canvases. The simple act of blending colors and forming shapes brought him serenity, a much-needed antidote to the hustle of his earlier life. Rajiv found not

SMOKE DANCES.... THOUGHTS WONDER
Medium: Acrylic Colour : Size: 12 x 16 Inch

ENLIGHTENMENT BLOOMS
Medium: Oil & Acrylic Colour : Size: 12 x 16 Inch

just beauty in the act of painting but also a profound connection with his inner self, uncovering dimensions of his personality that had remained unexplored.

His artistic journey, however, was not without its share of challenges. The path was peppered with moments of doubt, frustration and creative blocks. Today, Rajiv's work is a vibrant amalgamation of emotions and personal narratives. His bold use of colors and intricate details mirror his growth, his reflections and the ever-expanding horizons of his imagination. As he delves deeper into this new world, Rajiv continues to experiment with diverse techniques and styles, unafraid to push the boundaries of his creativity. Painting for Rajiv is more than a pastime— it's a meditative practice, a source of immense joy and areflection to the power of reinvention. Rajiv's journey is an inspiring reminder that age is no barrier to passion and retirement is not an end, but a new beginning. With every stroke, he proves that the brightest hues of life often emerge when we dare to embrace the unknown. In this vibrant second innings, Rajiv Kapoor is painting not just pictures, but a legacy of resilience, reinvention and boundless creativity.

JYOTI PRASAD
Jamtara, Jharkhand

Painting had always been more than a hobby—it had been a calling deeply ingrained in the soul, a gift inherited through generations. The journey as an art teacher began in 2011 with an appointment at Kendriya Vidyalaya. The first posting was at Kendriya Vidyalaya Jamalpur in the Patna region and later, talents were nurtured at Kendriya Vidyalaya Jamtara, Jharkhand under the Ranchi region. Over the years, countless children had been guided and mentored in the field of art, helping their creativity and imagination flourish. The academic journey included earning a Master's degree in Fine Arts from Chandigarh University, along with a graduation in Political Science from Bhagalpur University and an M.A. in Political Science from IGNOU. Additionally, several opportunities to serve as a judge in art competitions had further strengthened the passion for creativity. Faced with the choice of pursuing a conventional career or establishing a unique identity in painting, art had been chosen as a lifelong pursuit. This decision stemmed from the belief that art had the extraordinary ability to communicate emotions, heal minds and inspire change.

PEACE IN THE LAP OF NATURE : Medium : Acrylic : Size : 120 x 72 Inch

A GLIMPSE OF GOD IN MEDITATION : Medium : Acrylic : Size : 24 x 18 Inch

Through art, stories could be unveiled, emotions expressed and a canvas of hope and imagination painted. Art proved itself a profound medium with impacts on emotional, mental and physical health, while also fostering an understanding of history, culture and self-expression. To share this passion with others, a YouTube channel, Unique Art Universe, had been created, offering young artists a platform to explore and develop their talents. Firstly, I have made a nature painting which title is Peace in the lap of nature.I have tried to show a very calm, beautiful and healthy environment. Here two peacocks are sitting on a tree, a peacock and a peahen, who are talking to each other. A glimpse of God in meditation. In this painting, I have tried to show a glimpse of a devotee of God who, while walking on the true path and meditating, is able to see a glimpse of God for a few moments with the eyes of his inner mind. And in that moment, the devotee attains the infinite happiness of his life.

DR. KUKIL SHARMA
Guwahati, Assam

Hailing from the vibrant city of Guwahati, Assam, Dr. Kukil Sharma has emerged as a distinguished artist with a multitude of prestigious accolades to his name. Among his many honors are the International Icon Award 2024, Asia Icon Award, National Talent Honor, London Book of World Records 2024 and Bharat Shree Rastriya Saman 2024.

His remarkable journey also includes recognition with the National Best Artist Award, Best Artist Great Indian Parliament Award, Legendary Peace Award and the Golden Globe Oscar Award 2024, Sharad Shrestha Samman, Onyx Prestige award, Bharat Bhushan award 2024 , Achivers Book Of Records, Asia Rising Star Awards 2024 , Bharat Bhushan national award 2024, U.P Achivers award 2025, Dr. From American meri counsil into name just a few.

Beyond his remarkable

MAA KAALI
Medium : Oil Pastel : Size : 12 x 16 Inch

KRISHANA
Medium : Acrilic Colour on Canvas : Size : 16 x 16 Inch

achievements, Dr. Kukil Sharma holds a Doctorate from the Legendary Peace Award Council, further cementing his place in the global art community. His artistry and dedication have earned him the Nation's Pride Award and the title of Best Artist Personality of the Year. Dr. Kukil attributes his success to his parents, whose unwavering support and encouragement have been the cornerstone of his journey. From the very beginning, his mother ensured his participation in numerous competitions, while his father made sure he faced no obstacles in achieving his dreams. Together, they have been the driving force behind his extraordinary accomplishments. For those looking to follow his journey, you can connect with him on Instagram at Kukil_sharma. Dr. Kukil Sharma's story is one of immense talent, hard work and a deep gratitude for his family—a truereflection to the power of passion and perseverance.

MANDIRA GANGULY
Kolkata, West Bengal

In the picturesque town of Digboi, Assam, a young visionary embarked on an artistic journey destined for greatness. Painting was her language of emotions, a passion she nurtured for over a decade. Yet, it was only when she ventured beyond her hometown that her artistry truly flourished. Relocating to Kolkata, she completed her education before a transformative trip to Paris, France, at twenty-three. There, she attended the American Centre of Art, explored the Louvre and traversed Europe's finest museums. Under an inspiring mentor, she absorbed the essence of legendary masterpieces, shaping her artistic evolution.

Her pursuit of excellence led her to Swar Sangam at Birla Academy of Fine Arts and Culture. She participated in numerous group exhibitions and five solo showcases, earning two prestigious Art Excellence Awards. Her work, featured in esteemed publications,

FIRST SIGHTING : Medium : Acrylic on Canvas : Size : 36 x 30 Inch

A LEAP OF FAITH : Medium : Acrylic on Canvas : Size : 36 x 30 Inch

established her as a distinguished artist. During the pandemic, painting became her solace, exploring spirituality, nature and celestial wonders. Her impressionistic and symbolic compositions invite viewers into alternate realms. Her dedication earned her the Vande Mataram Award 2024 by Anuragyam, New Delhi. Her solo exhibition at Tribe Cafe Art Space in November was widely appreciated, with three paintings acquired by collectors. She showcased at Artverse's Birla Academy exhibition, graced by Munmun Sen and at RKM in 2024. Ten of her paintings were selected for a solo online exhibition by Bangia Kala Kendra, earning her a special certificate for outstanding artistic contribution. With each brushstroke, she narrates a story. Her journey is far from over—it is the beginning of a lasting artistic legacy.

KRISHAN KUMAR
Fatehabad, Haryana

Hailing from the quaint village of Alika in Fatehabad, Haryana, Krishan Kumar is an artist whose journey is as inspiring as his creations. A Bachelor of Fine Arts (BFA) graduate from Guru Kashi University, Bathinda and currently pursuing a B.Ed from Tirupati College of Education, Ratia, his passion for art transcends mere skill—it is a reflection of his soul. Born into a humble background with no familial ties to the world of art, Krishan's innate talent found its way onto paper from an early age. Having witnessed poverty firsthand, he channeled his emotions into evocative paintings that capture raw human emotions and societal realities. Every stroke on his canvas tells a story, often inspired by melancholy figures and social issues, igniting conversations through his work. His artistic journey began with his first award in 2017 on the occasion of Children's Day at the district level. Since then, he

SARDAR SOBHA SINGH
Medium: Paper with Water Colour : Size: A3 (11.7 x 16.5 Inch)

VILLAGE CULTURE
Medium: Paper with Water Colour : Size: 18.11 x 24.01 Inch

has amassed over 75 national and international accolades, including the Swami Vivekananda Youth Icon Award 2025 and the Vande Mataram Award 2025. In June 2021, he etched his name in the International Book of Records for creating the world's smallest Madhubani paintings. Krishan has won more than 75 award including International, National, State and District - level honours. Beyond his personal achievements, Krishan Kumar is a dedicated mentor. During the COVID-19 lockdown, he established Lalit Kala Academy Alika, providing free art education to children. His students have gone on to win over 55 awards at various levels, a reflection to his commitment to nurturing future artists. Guided by his mentor Krishan Singh ji Ratia, he draws inspiration from legendary artists like Leonardo da Vinci, Pablo Picasso, Amrita Shergil and M.F. Hussain. A lover of watercolors and poster colors, his works breathe life into everyday realities. His artistic pursuits extend beyond painting to music, drama, sculpture, choreography, photography and travel. For Krishan Kumar, black is not just a color—it is an emotion, a depth and a silent storyteller of life's beauty in simplicity. His art is not just seen; it is felt.

DR. DHRUVA TIWARI
Raipur, Chhattisgarh

Dr. Dhruva Tiwari is an internationally recognized artist from Raipur, Chhattisgarh, He servied as an art educator at Kendriya Vidyalaya No. 1 in Raipur. He completed his Bachelor of Fine Arts (BFA) and Master of Fine Arts (MFA) in Creative Painting from Indira Kala Sangeet Vishwavidyalaya, Khairagarh. He earned a doctoral degree focusing on the folk arts of Bastar. His paintings were exhibited at so many galleries. His paintings were exhibited at the art gallery in Raipur's Swami Vivekananda Airport. One of the exhibition featured ten of his works, highlighting Bastar's memory pillars, tribal culture and the diverse terrains of Chhattisgarh. This display offered travelers a glimpse into the state's rich heritage and received widespread appreciation. Dr. Tiwari has contributed to institutions such as Bharat Bhavan's Roopankar Department in Bhopal and the Indira Gandhi Rashtriya Manav Sangrahalaya. He has also served in the art departments of Delhi Public School Bhilai and Navodaya Vidyalaya Churhat. As a master trainer with NCERT, he has provided training to art educators across various cities, including Mumbai, Mysore and Gwalior.

CREATIVE LANDSCAPE
Medium: Acrylic Colors on Canvas : Size: 30 x 24 Inch

Anuragyam | Coffee Table Book | February 2025

Dr. Taruna Mathur, a TGT Art Educator at Kendriya Vidhyalay Sangathan residing in Vadodara, Gujarat. Originally from Jaipur, Rajasthan, Dr. Taruna Mathur is a landscape artist with a passion for creating stunning pieces inspired by nature. Dr. Taruna Mathur has become a versatile personality and a motivational speaker, inspiring countless individuals with her words of wisdom. Join Dr. Taruna Mathur on her journey as she continues to inspire, teach and create beautiful pieces of art that celebrate the beauty of nature. Her latest exhibitions were held at K.P. Campus in Ahmedabad, organized by the Canning Vale Markets in Perth, Australia, at MHRDM in New Delhi, by the G.P. Foundation Art Gallery in Lucknow and at the UDAAN Charitable Trust Painting Exhibition in Godhra, organized by Magnum Opus Art Gallery in Delhi. She has also participated in the MANU – The Power of Women Art Exhibition in Jhansi and many more. Dr. Taruna Mathur's paintings are a sight to behold and have garnered praise from all who have seen them.

DR. TARUNA MATHUR
Vadodara, Gujarat

MOHENJO-DARO
Medium: Acrylic Colors on Canvas : Size: 36 x 24 Inch

Our Art & Artist Coffee Table Books

Edition 1   :   Beyond Thinking
No. of Artists   :   25
No. of Artwork :   50
Year of Publish :   2022
Available at Amazon, Flipkart & Notion Press

Edition 2   :   Artistic Thinking
No. of Artists   :   25
No. of Artwork :   50
Year of Publish :   2023
Available at Amazon, Flipkart & Notion Press

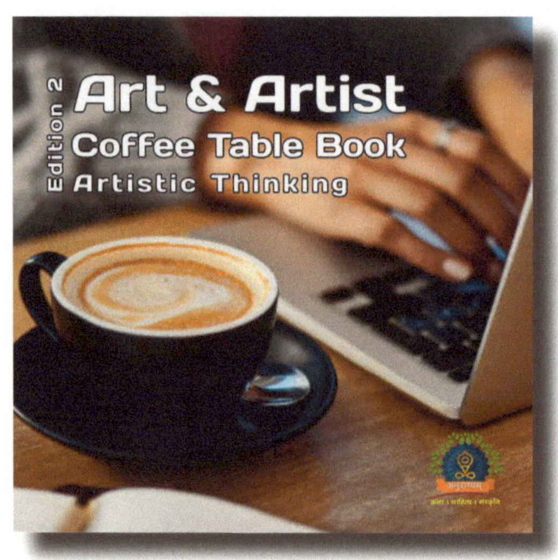

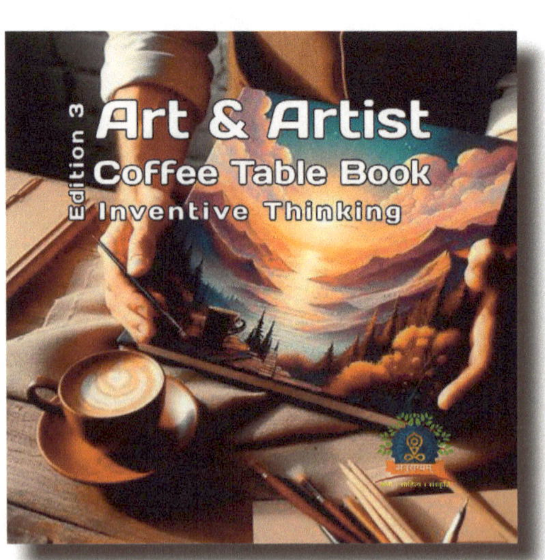

Edition 1   :   Inventive Thinking
No. of Artists   :   25
No. of Artwork :   50
Year of Publish :   2024
Available at Amazon, Flipkart & Notion Press

We Published Individual Artist Books

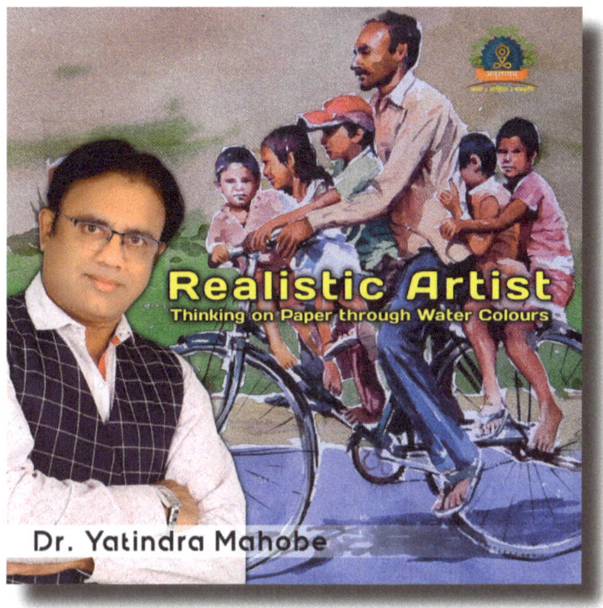

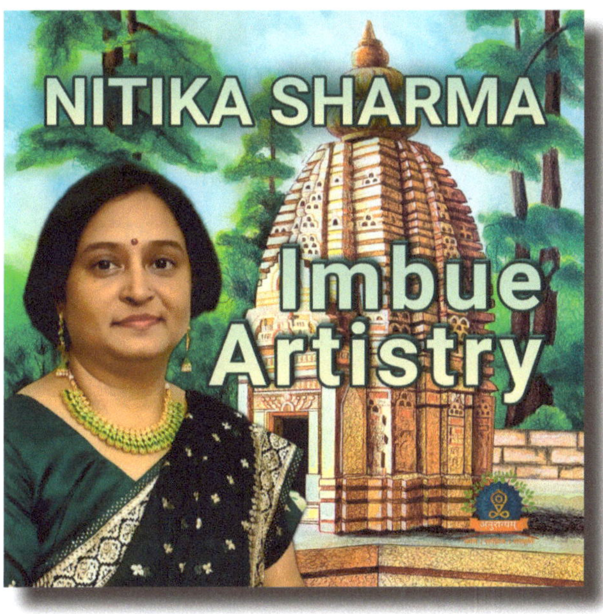

We Awarded Artists for their Artistic Journey.

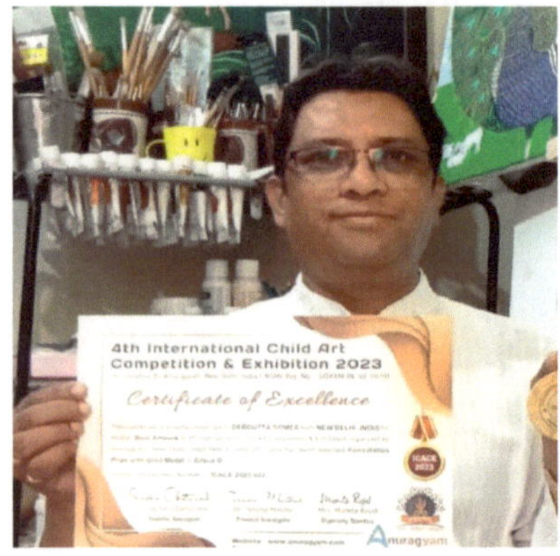